Lighthouse Keeper Cookbook

By Tim Murphy

**For information on Flannel John's
Cookbooks for Guys and Popped
Culture Cookbooks visit
www.flanneljohn.com**

The Lighthouse Keeper's Cookbook

TABLE OF CONTENTS

RECIPES

ABALONE CHOWDER

6 thin abalone fillets, diced
3 cups of milk
1½ cup of hot water
4 slices of bacon, diced
1 potato, peeled and diced
1 onion, diced fine
1 tablespoon of butter
Salt and pepper to taste

In a large pan, cook bacon until halfway crisp. Drain off all but 2 tablespoon of the bacon grease. Add the diced fish, potato and onion to the pan until all are browned. Add hot water and simmer until potatoes are tender. In a second pan heat milk and butter then combine both mixtures. Stir and warm and add salt and pepper to taste.

BACON, CHEESE & ALE SOUP

1 quart of chicken stock
12 ounces of ale
6 ounces of cheddar cheese, grated
4 strips of thick-cut peppered bacon
½ cup of onion, diced
¼ cup of all-purpose flour
½ teaspoon of pepper, black or white
Salt to taste

Brown the bacon in a pan and pour off the grease. Add onion and butter and cook for 5 minutes over medium heat. Sprinkle in the flour and stir to thicken. Cook for 3 minutes. Add in the stock, ale and cheese and season with salt and pepper to taste. Continue to cook until cheese is melted and all is thoroughly heated.

BAKED BEAN SOUP

16 ounces of baked beans with molasses
15 ounces of stewed tomatoes w/ juice, diced
14 ounces of beef broth
1 tablespoon of onion, minced
Salt and pepper to taste

Combine all of the ingredients in a lightly greased slow cooker. Cover and cook on low heat for 4 to 6 hours.

BAKED HALIBUT

½ pound of halibut fillets
½ stick of butter
Salt and pepper to taste

Place fish in a greased baking dish. Salt and pepper to taste. Slowly melt the butter in a small pan. Baste the fish with the butter. Bake at 350 degrees for 20 to 25 minutes. Baste the fish a few times during baking.

BAKED WALLEYE

½ pound of walleye fillets
4 ounces of mushroom pieces, canned
2 tablespoons of sour cream
2 tablespoons of mayonnaise
¼ stick of butter
Salt and pepper to taste

Place the fish in a greased baking dish. Combine remaining ingredients thoroughly and spread over the fish. Bake at 350 degrees for 20 to 25 minutes.

BEER STEW

2½ pounds of beef or chuck roast, cubed
16 ounces of beer
¼ cup + 2 tablespoons of flour
1 onion, diced
2 cloves of garlic, minced
4 carrots, diced large
2 stalks of celery, diced large
4 tablespoons of butter, melted
2 tablespoons of tomato paste
2½ teaspoons of salt
1½ teaspoons or oregano
½ teaspoon of pepper

In a slow cooker combine beef, beer, onion, garlic, carrots, celery, salt, pepper, oregano and tomato paste. Cook on low for 9 hours. Combine melted butter and flour to form a smooth paste. Stir this into the cooker. Raise heat to high to thicken the stew just before serving.

BLOODY MARY VENISON ROAST

3 pound venison roast
3 cups of Bloody Mary Mix
Pepper to taste (optional)
Tabasco to taste (optional)

Put the venison roast in a slow cooker and cover with the Bloody Mary mix. Add optional seasonings. Cover the cooker with a lid or a foil tent to keep the meat moist. Cook on low heat for 6 to 8 hours.

BREAD PUDDING

2 cups of milk
2 cups of bread cubes
2 eggs
3 tablespoons of butter
½ cup of raisins
¼ cup of sugar
½ teaspoon of vanilla
¼ teaspoon of nutmeg
Pinch of salt

Combine milk, butter and sugar in a pan and heat just before boiling. Beat eggs slightly and sprinkle in salt. Stir the eggs and vanilla into the milk mixture slowly. Add in nutmeg and raisins. Pour bread cubes into a lightly greased baking dish and pour the milk mixture over the bread. Place baking dish in container of warm water. The water level should match the pudding level. Bake at 350 degrees for 1 hour.

BREAKFAST CASSEROLE

1 pound of link sausage
2¼ cups of milk
1 can of cream of mushroom
½ can of milk
8 slices of bread, cubed
8 ounces of can mushrooms, chopped
½ pound of Cheddar cheese, grated
5 eggs
2 tablespoons of butter
¾ teaspoon of dry mustard

In a greased baking dish distribute bread cubes evenly. Cut the sausage into bit-sized pieces and brown in a skillet. Cover bread with cheese and sausage pieces. Beat eggs with milk and mustard, combine with mushrooms and pour over everything. Cover and refrigerate overnight. Take out of fridge for 1 hour. Combine milk and soup and pour over the top then dot with butter. Bake at 325 degrees for 1 hour.

BURGOO

16 ounces of canned whole-kernel corn
16 ounces of canned baby lima beans, drained
14 ounces of stewed tomatoes, diced
   (save the juice)
10 ounces of double-strength chicken broth
1 pound of beef stew meat, cubed
1 pound of pork stew meat, cubed
4 chicken thighs, skinned
1 cup of green pepper, chopped
3 carrots, diced
2 read potatoes, peeled and cubed
1 onion, diced
1 teaspoon of onion salt
½ teaspoon of pepper
¼ teaspoon of ground red pepper

Place the beef and pork in a slow cooker. Sprinkle onion salt, pepper and red pepper. Mix until coated. Layer cooker with carrots, onion, chicken, potatoes, green peppers, stewed tomatoes with juice. Pour liquid from canned corn into the pot and set corn aside. Cover and cook on high for 4 hours or on low for 8½ hours until beef, pork and vegetables are tender. Remove chicken and stir in corn and lima beans. Cook on high for 30 minutes. Remove chicken from the bone and cut into small pieces. Return the meat to the mixture and heat thoroughly.

BUTTERMILK PANCAKES

2¼ cups of buttermilk
2 cups of sifted flour
2 eggs
2 tablespoons of butter or margarine, melted
   (bacon grease is an option)
1 teaspoon of baking soda
1 teaspoon of salt

Sift flour, baking soda and salt together in a bowl. Blend in eggs and buttermilk slowly. Stir until the batter is smooth. Stir in butter. Drop spoonfuls onto a hot, lightly greased griddle or skillet.

CANADIAN CHEESE SOUP

2 cups of Cheddar cheese, cubed
2 cups of milk
2 cups of water
2 carrots, diced
2 stalks of celery, diced
2 chicken bouillon cubes
¼ cup of flour

Put water, carrots, celery and bouillon cubs in a blender. Pulse the blender until vegetables are finely chopped. Pour into a pot and heat until tender. Put cheese, milk and flour in the blender and blend until smooth. Add cheese mixture to the vegetables. Heat and stir until thick and hot.

CRAB CAKES

1 cup of crab
8 saltine crackers, crushed fine
1 tablespoon of green onion, diced
1 tablespoon of celery, diced fine
1 tablespoon of mayonnaise
1 teaspoon of Worcestershire sauce
½ teaspoon of mustard
½ teaspoon of seafood seasoning

In a bowl, combine all of the ingredients thoroughly and form into patties. In a skillet, fry the patties in oil or butter.

CRAB CASSEROLE

6 ounces of crabmeat
4 ounces of mushroom pieces, canned
1 can of cream of mushroom soup
1 cup of peas, cooked
1 cup of fresh breadcrumbs

Mix the first 4 ingredients thoroughly in a greased baking dish. Sprinkle with breadcrumbs and bake at 350 degrees for 30 minutes.

CRAB QUICHE

2 cups of crabmeat, shredded
2 cups of Cheddar cheese, shredded
1 cups of Swiss cheese, shredded
¾ cup of Parmesan cheese, grated
1 cup of milk
½ cup of whipping cream
2 eggs, beaten
Unbaked piecrust, 9-inch in diameter

Combine crab with Cheddar cheese and Swiss cheese thoroughly. Pour into the piecrust. Combine milk, cream eggs and Parmesan cheese thoroughly and pour over the pie filling. Bake at 350 degrees for 1 hour.

CRABMEAT & BACON ROLLS

1 cup of crabmeat
8 slices of bacon, cut in half
½ cup of fine dry bread crumbs
¼ cup of tomato juice
1 egg, well beaten
1 tablespoon of parsley, chopped
1 tablespoon of lemon juice
¼ teaspoon of salt
¼ teaspoon of Worcestershire sauce
Dash of pepper

Mix egg and tomato sauce thoroughly. Add in remaining ingredients except the bacon. Mix thoroughly and form into 16 rolls about 2 inches long. Wrap each with a half slice of bacon and secure with a toothpick. Broil 5 inches from heat for 8 to 10 minutes. Turn often to brown evenly.

DUNGENESS CRAB

2 live Dungeness crabs, 3 to 4 pounds each
¼ cup + 2 tablespoons of melted butter
¼ cup of Old Bay Seasoning
1 tablespoon of paprika
½ teaspoon of cayenne pepper
Beer
Water

Place the live crabs on ice. Partially fill the bottom of a steamer with an equal mixture of water and beer. Thoroughly mix the Old Bay, paprika and cayenne. Place the crabs on the steamer rack and sprinkle with seasoning mixture over the crabs and legs, holding back 1 teaspoon. Cover and steam for 20 minutes over medium-high heat. Mix the remaining spices with the melted butter and use for dipping the crabmeat.

EMPTY WOODS CHILI
(No Meat – Just Veggies and Beans)

28 ounces of red kidney beans, canned
½ cup of dried lentils
1 tablespoon of olive oil
1 onion, chopped and peeled
1 red pepper chopped with no seeds
1½ cloves of garlic crushed
14 ounces of canned tomatoes
1 teaspoon of paprika
2 tablespoons of chili powder
Salt and black pepper
¼ teaspoon of sugar

Simmer lentils and beans in water for 40 to 45 minutes, until tender. Heat oil in a large pan and sauté onion and pepper for 10 minutes. Add in garlic and cook for 1 to 2 minutes and then add tomatoes. Drain the beans and lentils, reserving the liquid. Add beans and lentils to the tomato mixture with the chili powder and paprika. Simmer for 15 minutes, pouring in the bean water as needed for consistency. Season and add sugar.

FIDDLEHEAD SOUP

3 cups of milk
1 cup of chicken broth
1 cup of fiddleheads
1 cup of fresh mushrooms, sliced
¼ cup of flour
¾ cup of leeks (just the white part)
¼ cup of green onions, diced
½ cup of butter, in pieces
1 teaspoon of lemon juice
½ teaspoon of salt
Pinch of cayenne pepper

In a pot, melt the butter. Sauté the fiddleheads, mushrooms, leeks and onions for 4 to 5 minutes or until tender. Slowly stir in flour, salt and cayenne pepper. Gradually add in the milk and broth until blended. Mix thoroughly and bring to a light boil for 10 minutes or until it thickens. Reduce the heat and simmer for 10 minutes or until thoroughly heated. Stir in lemon juice just before you remove it from the heat.

FISH AND CATTAILS

2 quarts of cattail shoots or young stems,
  washed
4 bass or trout fillets
2 cups of water
Salt to taste
Crushed red pepper, to taste

Harvest spring cattail shoots or green, new stems. Put fish fillets in a skillet and lay cattails on tops. Pour water into the skillet and cover. Steam for 5 to 10 minutes. Season to taste with salt and crushed red pepper.

FISH CASSEROLE

8 ounces of fish, cleaned and diced
1 cup of fresh breadcrumbs
2 eggs, beaten
½ cup of Half & Half
1 tablespoon of parsley flakes
1 teaspoon of onion flakes
½ teaspoon of salt

Combine all of the ingredients in a lightly greased baking dish. Bake at 350 degrees for 30 minutes.

FISH CHOWDER

1 pound of fish fillets, cleaned
2½ cups of potatoes, diced
2 cups of milk
1½ cups of boiling water
2 tablespoons of bacon, chopped and cooked
1 tablespoon of butter
1 teaspoon of salt
Pepper to taste

In a pot fry bacon until crisp then stir in onion and cook until tender. Add potatoes, water, seasonings and fish. Cover and simmer for 15 to 20 minutes or until potatoes are tender. Add milk and butter and continue to heat.

FISH WITH GARLIC BUTTER

6 fish fillets
4 cloves of garlic, crushed
½ cup of butter
½ cup of lime juice
2 teaspoons of salt
¼ teaspoon of pepper
¼ teaspoon of hot sauce

In a pan, lightly brown garlic in the butter. Add lime juice, hot sauce, salt and pepper and stir. Place fish in a baking dish. Pour sauce over the fish. Broil until fish turns slightly brown while basting occasionally. You can also bake at 375 degrees for 18 to 24 minutes depending on the fish.

FISH HEAD STEW

1 salmon head
1 skein of salmon row
½ piece of salmon backbone
5 chunks of salmon
1 salmon tail
4 potatoes, peeled and diced
2 cups of celery, diced
1 onion, diced
1 can of corn
Salt and pepper to taste
Water

Put salmon head, salmon row, celery, onion, potato, salmon chunks, salmon backbone, corn and salmon tail in a stew pot. Add in enough water to cover 2 inches above the ingredients. Boil until potatoes and fish are done. Salt and pepper to taste. Watch out for small bones.

FISH WITH DANDELIONS

2 trout, salmon or bass
6 handfuls of dandelion greens
3 wild onions
2 pinches of white sage
1 lemon
Bacon grease
Salt and pepper to taste

Cut and clean the fish. Then cut the fish into long strips. Dice the onion and thinly slice the lemon. Wash and chop the dandelion leaves. Grease a skillet with bacon grease and put on medium heat. Add fish strips, onion, 6 thin slices of lemon, salt, pepper and white sage to the skillet. Cook until ingredients are 75% done then add the dandelion leaves. Cook until leaves are soft. Add salt, pepper and white sage again. Just before serving drizzle with lemon juice. If ingredients stick to the skillet, add in a little more bacon grease. The fish should brown just a bit.

FISH WITH VEGETABLES

½ pound of fish fillets
½ cup of onion, diced
½ cup of celery, diced
½ cup of tomatoes, diced
½ cup of mushrooms, sliced
½ cup of zucchini, sliced
½ stick of butter
2 tablespoons of lemon juice
Salt and pepper to taste

In a skillet sauté the vegetables with butter until tender. Add in remaining ingredients, cover and simmer until the fish flakes.

FIVE-GRAIN PANCAKES

2 cups of buttermilk
1 cup of sour cream
1 cup of flour
¼ cup of rye flour
¼ cup of soy meal flour
¼ cup of buckwheat flour
¼ cup of cornmeal
¼ cup of bran cereal
2 eggs
2 tablespoons of sugar
½ teaspoon of salt
2 teaspoons of baking soda
¼ cup of arm water

In a bowl thoroughly mix buttermilk, sour cream, eggs, salt and sugar. Stir in the bran cereal to the mixture. Sift the four flours and cornmeal together and add to the wet mixture. Dissolve the baking soda in ¼ cup of warm water. Add the baking soda water to the batter. Spoon the batter onto a hot lightly greased griddle or skillet. Flip the pancakes after a few minutes.

FOG HORN CHILI

2 pounds of ground beef (elk or venison)
2 pounds of tomatoes, diced (fresh or canned)
1 onion, diced
1 bell pepper, diced
6 ounces of tomato paste
1 cup of water
1 can of kidney beans
½ teaspoon of garlic powder
2 teaspoons of salt
2 teaspoons of Italian seasoning
2 teaspoons of chili powder
2 teaspoons of pepper

Brown the meat in a skillet. Put the meat and the rest of the ingredients in a pot. Cover and simmer at a low temperature for 45 to 60 minutes.

FRESH MOREL MUSHROOMS

1 pound of fresh morel mushrooms,
   trimmed and sliced
1 cup of beef sock
½ cup of heavy cream
3 tablespoons of butter
2 shallots, peeled and minced
Salt and fresh ground pepper to taste

In a skillet, heat the butter and sauté the shallots for 5 minutes until they soften. Add the remaining ingredients and cook over medium-high heat for 10 minutes or until the sauce thickens. Season with salt and pepper

FRIED OYSTERS

2 pints of oysters
4 tablespoons of butter
4 tablespoons of oil
4 whole eggs
2 cups of flour or dry breadcrumbs
Pepper to taste
Garlic powder to taste
Onion powder to taste
2 tablespoons of cold water

Drain oysters completely. Mix flour or breadcrumbs with pepper, garlic powder and onion powder. In a bowl beat eggs with 2 tablespoons of cold water. Dip oyster in the egg mixture then press into dry mixture of flour or breadcrumbs. Place on a cookie sheet to rest for 30 minutes. In a pan mix oil and butter over medium heat. Put oysters in the pan and fry until edges curl slightly and they turn golden brown. This should take 2 ½ to 3 minutes per side. Be careful not to overcook and do it in small batches. When you're don, place oysters on paper towel to drain excess oil. If this recipe makes more than you need, cut all ingredient amounts in half.

FRIED PERCH

1 pound of perch, cut into 1-inch pieces
1 cup of flour
1 cup of warm beer (not dark)
1 tablespoon of dry yeast
½ teaspoon of salt
24 ounces of oil (if using a deep fryer)

Mix yeast, flour and salt with ½ cup of the beer and stir until smooth. Add the remainder of the beer and continue to stir until smooth. Let batter stand fort 30 minutes and stir batter again. Dip perch into batter and deep fry in oil at 350 degrees. If using a skillet, fry in oil on medium to high heat until golden brown.

FRIED RAZOR CLAMS

2 pounds of razor clams, prepped for cooking
2 tablespoons of butter
¼ cup of oil
¾ cup of four
½ teaspoon of salt
¼ teaspoon of pepper

In a large skillet heat butter and oil until medium hot. Combine flour, salt and pepper thoroughly and dredge the clams in the mixture. Fry clams in the hot oil for 1 to 2 minutes.

GARLIC & PARSLEY BUTTER

½ cup of butter, melted
2 cloves of garlic, crushed
2 tablespoons of parsley, chopped

Melt the butter slowly in a pan and stir in the garlic
and parsley. Stir until well mixed

GREAT LAKES STEW

1½ pounds of beef, cubed
½ pound of mushrooms
½ cup of water
1 package of dry onion soup mix
1 package of mushroom gravy mix
1 cup of apple juice or dry red wine
6 carrots, diced
3 potatoes, diced
Pepper to taste

Put the beef in a baking or casserole dish. Combine soup mix, gravy mix, pepper, wine and water and mix thoroughly. Pour over the beef and stir. Cover the dish and bake at 350 degrees for 1 hour. Add the vegetables and mix thoroughly. Cover and bake for 90 minutes.

GRILLED STEELHEAD

4 steelhead fillets, 1-inch thick
¼ cup of oil
¼ cup of soy sauce
2 cloves of garlic, minced
3 tablespoons of parsley
Pepper to taste

Combine oil, parsley, garlic, soy sauce and pepper into a marinade. Soak the fish in the liquid for 1 to 2 hours in the fridge. Drain the marinade and save. Grill over medium-hot coals for 6 to 8 minutes flip and grill for another 6 to 8 minutes Baste fish occasionally with marinade. It can also be baked in a baking dish at 350 degrees for 18 to 22 minutes. Baste occasionally.

GRILLED TROUT

2 pounds of trout (or fillets of choice)
¼ cup of French dressing
1 tablespoon of lemon juice
1 tablespoon of grated onion
2 teaspoons of salt
Pepper to taste

Cut cleaned fillets into chunks. Combine remaining ingredients and mix thoroughly. Baste the fish chunks in the sauce and grill over hot coals for 6 to 8 minutes and turn. Alternate methods include putting fish in foil packets and cooking near coals for 15 minutes or put fish in a skillet and cook over medium high heat for 15 to 20 minutes until the fish flakes easily.

GULF COAST CHICKEN

4 chicken breasts, skinless & boneless
1 can of cream of chicken coup
16 ounces of chunky salsa

Put the chicken breasts in a greased slow cooker. Thoroughly combine soup and salsa in bowl and pour the mixture over the chicken. Cover and cook on low for 6 to 8 hours.

HOT BUTTERED APPLE CIDER

16 ounces of apple cider
½ cup of real maple syrup
½ cup of softened butter
½ teaspoon of ground nutmeg
½ teaspoon of ground allspice

Combine apple cider and maple syrup in a slow cooker and cook over low heat for 20 minutes until steaming. In a bowl, mix butter, nutmeg and allspice thoroughly. Pour the cider into mugs and top with a dollop of the spices butter.

HUNTING PARTY SOUP

1 pound of venison, diced large and cooked
4 cups of broth, beef or vegetable
3 stalks of celery, diced
2 potatoes, peeled and diced large
2 carrots, diced
Salt and pepper to taste

In a large pot or Dutch oven, combine broth and vegetables. Bring to a boil and reduce heat. Simmer for 15 minutes or until vegetables are tender. Add cooked venison cubes and simmer for 12 to 15 minutes.

LAMB STEW

2 pounds of lean lamb shoulder, cubed
2 quarts of beef stock
2 onions, diced
2 potatoes, peeled and diced
1 cup of sour cream
½ cup of fresh green beans, sliced
¼ cup of butter
2 bay leaves
1 tablespoon of flour
1 tablespoon of paprika
Salt and pepper to taste

In a pan, sauté onions in the butter. While cooking, add the lamb and brown. Stir in the paprika and heat for 1 minute. Pour all of the ingredients from the pan into a slow cooker and add beef stock, bay leaves, salt and pepper. Cook on low for 7 hours. Add potatoes and green beans and cook for an additional 2½ hours. 30 minutes before serving combine flour and sour cream thoroughly and slowly stir into soup.

LEMON PEPPER OYSTERS

2 dozen oysters, as fresh as possible
1 lemon, cut into wedges
Freshly ground pepper

Leave oysters on a half shell with liquid. Sprinkle each with fresh ground pepper with lemon wedges on the side.

LENTIL SOUP

4 cups of water
2 cups of tomato juice
1½ cups of dried lentils
½ cup of onion, diced
2 coves of garlic, minced
2 tablespoons of butter
1 teaspoon of salt
2 bay leaves
Dill sees to taste (optional)

Melt butter in a pot. Sauté onion and garlic in the butter until tender. Rinse and drain lentils. Add water and lentils to a slow cooker and cook on low heat for 4 hours. Add tomato juice, salt, bay leaves and dill seed. Cook for an additional 2 to 3 hours.

LOBSTER SAUCE

10 ounces of lobster soup, canned
5 ounces of cream
1 tablespoon of butter

Thoroughly mix the lobster soup with cream until smooth. Add in the butter and heat to just before boiling.

MINT TEA

10 fresh mint leaves, clean and rinsed
2 cups of water
Lemon to taste
Sugar to taste

Boil the water in a pot. After rinsing the leaves, tear them to release the aroma and flavors. Remove the water from the heat and drop the leaves into the water either loosely or in a tea ball. Let steep for up to 10 minutes, depending on how stronger you want the flavor. Strain leaves or remove tea ball. Pour into a mug and add lemon and sugar to taste.

MOOSE SOUP

1 pound of moose meat
½ gallon of water
1 cup of rice
1 cup of macaroni
¼ cup of salt
¼ cup of dried onions

Cut and clean the moose meat. Put the moose meat, onions and salt in a pot with the water. When the pot starts to boil, turn the heat down and let it boil for 45 minutes. Add rice and macaroni to the pot and boil for 15 to 20 minutes. Then the soup will be done.

MULLED CIDER

2 quarts of fresh apple cider
½ cup of brown sugar
3 sticks of cinnamon
1 teaspoon of whole allspice
1 teaspoon of whole cloves
½ teaspoon of salt
Dash of grated nutmeg

Mix cider, salt and sugar in a pot. Tie spices up into a small cheesecloth bag and add to cider mixture. Slowly bring to a boil, cover and simmer for 15 to 20 minutes. Remove cheesecloth and serve.

NARAGANSETT CHOWDER

1 pound of salt cod, cubed
½ pound of salt pork, cubed
2 cups of potatoes, peeled and diced
2 cups of milk
2 bay leaves

In a pan, fry the pork until it starts to brown. Stir in remaining ingredients and slowly simmer until potatoes are tender.

NORTHERN PIKE

4 8-ounce Northern Pike fillets
1 cup of milk
1 green onion, diced fine
1 tablespoon of fresh parsley, diced fine
½ cup of butter, melted
½ cup of dry breadcrumbs
½ teaspoon of salt
½ teaspoon of pepper

Put fillets in a bowl with milk and soak for 30 minutes in the refrigerator. Mix breadcrumbs, salt, pepper and parsley thoroughly. Remove fish from milk and dredge in breadcrumb mixture until completely coated. Place fish in a lightly greased baking dish. Sprinkle green onion over fish and drizzle with melted butter. Bake at 350 degrees for 25 minutes or until fish flakes easily.

NORTHWEST CHOWDER

2 pounds of tomatoes, fresh preferably
2 pounds of halibut or fish of choice,
    cut into bite-sized chunks
8 cups of hot water
3 cups of potatoes, diced
1 ½ cups of carrots, diced
1 cup of onions, diced
1 cup of celery, diced
4 tablespoons of butter
2 teaspoons of salt
1 teaspoon of thymes
¼ teaspoon of pepper

Melt butter in a pot with onions and time. Cook until onions are tender. Add hot water, celery, potatoes, salt and pepper. Cover and simmer for 5 minutes. Add tomatoes and carrots. Simmer uncovered for 1 hour. Add fish chunks, cover and simmer for 30 minutes.

OMELET PIE

6 slices of cheese
8 eggs, beaten
6 slices of bacon, cooked, chopped & drained
¼ cup of milk
½ teaspoon of salt
¼ teaspoon of pepper

On a buttered 9-inch pie plate arrange the cheese slices. Beat the eggs and stir in milk, salt and pepper. Add bacon to the egg mixture and slowly pour into the pie plate. Bake at 350 degrees for 40 minutes.

OYSTER STEW

1 pint of oysters (the smaller the better)
  Reserve the juice
1 pint of whole milk
1 pint of cream
6 tablespoons of butter
Salt and pepper to taste
Paprika (optional)

In a pan met 2 tablespoons of butter. Add oyster juice and sauté until they swell and edges curl. In a second pan heat milk and cream but do not boil. Season the milk mixture with salt and pepper. Add oysters and juice to milk and continue to warm. When hot pour into 4 bowls and top with a tablespoon of butter and if you like, sprinkle with paprika.

OYSTERS ON THE HALF SHELL

2 dozen oysters
1 lemon, cut into wedges
Fresh ground pepper
Seaweed (optional, for presentation)

Put seaweed on a platter and gently nestle oysters on the half shell so they are held in place and do not lose their liquid. Sprinkle each oyster with fresh ground pepper. Garnish with lemon wedges. Serve fresh.

PAN FRIED BANNOCK

2 cups of flour
2 cups of water
1 cup of raisins
3 tablespoons of baking powder
1 tablespoon of lard, oil or butter
2 eggs (optional)
½ cup of sugar (optional)

Put the flour in a bowl and add baking powder. Stir it thoroughly. Add raisins and water and mix well. Put 1 tablespoon of lard into a skillet and melt it. Pour the bannock into pan and cook it. Rotate the bannock so it cooks evenly, check with a fork to see if it's cooked inside. Flip and cook on both sides. If you're camping you can leave out the eggs and sugar. It's quicker and easier.

PAN FRIED SMELT

½ pound of smelt
¾ cup of milk
¼ cup of flour
2 tablespoons of cornmeal
½ teaspoon of salt
¼ teaspoon of pepper
Oil

Heat oil in a skillet. Thoroughly mix flour, cornmeal, salt and pepper. Dip the smelt in milk and roll in the flour mixture. Fry fast and hot, browning both sides of the smelt.

PEPPERED TROUT

2 pounds of trout
2 cups of cooked tomatoes
2 cups of potato balls
1 cup of mushrooms
1 clove of garlic
1 red pepper pod
1 onion, minced
½ cup of olive oil
1 tablespoon of Worcestershire sauce
1 tablespoon of vinegar
Salt and pepper to taste

Sprinkle trout with salt and pepper. Put garlic and pepper pod inside the fish. Place onion and fish in a pan or baking dish and cover with tomatoes. Add Worcestershire sauce, vinegar, olive oil and potato balls. Bake at 400 degrees for 15 minutes. Add mushrooms and bake for an additional 15 minutes or until fish and potatoes are tender.

PORK CHOPS

4 pork chops, 1-inch thick
1 cup of water
1 cup of white wine
1 teaspoon of rosemary
½ teaspoon of sage
½ clove of garlic, chopped
Salt
Ground pepper
Oil

Combine rosemary, sage, garlic, salt and pepper. Rub down the chops with this mixture. Put chops in a skillet with a little bit of oil. Pour in water, cover and simmer until water evaporates. This should be 35 to 45 minutes. Remove the cover and brown the chops in their fat. Remove chops from the skillet and cook onion in the juice for 1 minute. Put chops back in the skillet with wine and cook until half the liquid evaporates then serve. Use liquid in the skillet as sauce if you like.

PORTLAND HEAD LIGHT CHOWDER

1 pound of fish fillets, cleaned
2½ cups of potatoes, diced
2 cups of milk
1½ cups of boiling water
2 tablespoons of bacon, chopped and cooked
1 tablespoon of butter
1 teaspoon of salt
Pepper to taste

In a pot fry bacon until crisp then stir in onion and cook until tender. Add potatoes, water, seasonings and fish. Cover and simmer for 15 to 20 minutes or until potatoes are tender. Add milk and butter and continue to heat.

POTATO SOUP

6 potatoes, peeled and diced
5 cups of water
1 can of evaporated milk
1/3 cup of butter
1 onion, diced
3 carrots, pared and sliced
1 stalk of celery, diced
4 chicken bouillon cubes
1 tablespoon of parsley flakes
1 tablespoon of salt
Pepper

Put all ingredients in a crock-pot except evaporated milk. Cover and cook on low heat for 10 to 12 hours. Stir in the evaporated milk during the last hour.

SALMON ON A STICK

Salmon or any available fish

Build a fire. Clean the fish and cut it in half or into meal-size chunks. Skewer the fish on a stick. Place the fish on a stick into the ground close to the hot coals. Turn the fish, as the bottom will cook quickly. Don't underestimate the speed at which the fish will cook on the stick. Season as you like.

SALMON WITH CHICKEN SAUCE

½ pound of salmon fillets
1 cup of chicken bouillon
½ cup of instant potato flakes
½ teaspoon of garlic powder

Poach the fish and keep warm. In a skillet mix chicken bouillon, garlic powder and potato thoroughly and heat. Stir until the liquid thickens. Pour over fish and serve.

SCALLOP CHOWDER

8 ounces of clam juice
2 cups of half & half
1 pound of scallops
1 onion, diced
1 red bell pepper, chopped
1 cup of red potato, chopped
½ cup of fresh parsley
½ cup of carrots, diced
½ cup of celery, chopped
2 tablespoons of butter
¼ teaspoon of oregano
¼ teaspoon of salt
¼ teaspoon of pepper

Melt butter in a large pan. Add onion, carrots, celery, bell pepper, potatoes and oregano. Sauté the mixture for 10 minutes. Pour in clam juice and scallops and cook for 5 minutes. Add half & half, salt and pepper and cook until thoroughly heated. Stir in parsley for a minute and serve.

SHINNECOCK SOUP

1 cup of fish, chunked
1 can of mushroom soup
1 can of cream of tomato soup
2 soup cans of water
2 tablespoons of butter
¼ teaspoon of paprika
¼ teaspoon of curry
¼ teaspoon of fish seasoning
¼ teaspoon of salt
Pepper to taste
Lemon slices

Pour soup into a pan. Stir in water, fish and seasonings. Heat and simmer for 10 minutes. Add butter to the pan and let it melt. Stir thoroughly. Ladle into bowls and float a lemon slice on each bowl.

SHORELINE CLAMBAKE

12 small onions, peeled
6 medium potatoes, washed
6 ears of corn in the husk
6 dozen clams, shells washed
6 live lobsters, 1 pound each (optional)
12 large pieces of cheesecloth
12 large pieces of aluminum foil

Start a campfire or fire up the grill. Put water a large pot and parboil the onions and potatoes for 15 minutes then drain. Remove the silk from the corn and pull husks back in place. Place 2 pieces of cheesecloth on top of 2 pieces of aluminum foil. Place 2 onions, 1 potato, 1 ear of corn, a dozen clams and 1 lobster (optional). Tie the opposite ends of the cheesecloth together. Pour 1 cup of water over the cheesecloth bundle and bring foil up over the package, closing the edges with double folds. Repeat until all 6 packages are done. Place packages on the grill or 4 inches from the hot coals. Cover with hood or aluminum foil if on a grill. Cook for 45 to 60 minutes or until potatoes and onions are tender.

SMOKED HAZELNUTS

2 cups of hazelnuts, shelled
2 tablespoons of butter, melted
¾ teaspoon of chili powder
¼ teaspoon of kosher salt
½ teaspoon of liquid smoke
Cayenne pepper to taste

Spread hazelnuts in a lipped cookie sheet or shallow pan. Roast at 275 degrees for 25 minutes until the skins crack. Remove skins from the hazelnuts. Combine butter, salt, chili powder, liquid smoke and cayenne pepper thoroughly. Mix the nuts and seasonings thoroughly. Put the nuts back on a cleaned cookie sheet or shallow pan and bake at 275 degrees for 10 minutes.

SMOKED OYSTER DIP

12 ounces of cream cheese, softened
4 ounces of smoked oysters with oil, canned
3 drops of Tabasco sauce
¼ teaspoon of onion powder (or to taste)

Put all ingredients in a food processor or blender. Blend until smooth. Chill for at least 2 hours before serving.

SOUTHAMPTON SOUP

2 cups of flaked or diced fish, cooked or raw
1 can of mushroom soup
1 can of asparagus soup
1 soup can of milk
1 soup can of water
2 tablespoons of sherry
2 tablespoons of butter

In a pan, blend all of the ingredients thoroughly then simmer for 10 minutes.

SPINACH & OYSTER SOUP

1 quart of 2% milk
1 quart of Half & Half
1 pound of shucked oyster with liquid
7 cups of spinach, rinsed
2 teaspoons of salt
Pepper to taste

In a large pot, combine milk and Half & Half and bring to a boil. In a smaller pan, sauté oysters in their liquid for 3 to 3 minutes. Put spinach on top of the oysters and continue to cook until leaves just begin to wilt. Puree spinach and oysters in a blender or food processor and stir in to the hot milk mixture. Stir and blend thoroughly. Season with salt and pepper.

SPLIT PEA & HAM SOUP

3 quarts of water
1 pound of dried split peas
1 smoked ham shank
1 cup of cooked ham, diced
4 slices of bacon, cooked and diced
1½ onions, diced
2 carrots, diced
2 stalks of celery, diced
½ teaspoon of cayenne pepper (optional)
2 bay leaves
Salt and pepper to taste

In a skillet fry the bacon until crisp. Remove from the pan and dice. Sauté onion, carrot and celery in the bacon grease for 5 minutes. Place all of the ingredients except diced ham into a slow cooker. Cook on low and cook for 8 to 9 hours or until peas are soft. Stir in diced ham just before serving and heat it thoroughly. Adjust flavor if needed with salt and pepper.

SUPERIOR SHORES CASSEROLE

3 cups of chicken broth
1 cup of wild rice
8 ounces of mushrooms, sliced
½ cup of sunflower seeds, hulled
¼ cup of butter
3 tablespoons of shallots, minced
1 teaspoon of Worcestershire sauce
1 bay leaf

Rinse rice in cold running water. In a baking or casserole dish, combine rice, broth, mushrooms, sunflower seeds, shallots, Worcestershire sauce and bay leaf and mix thoroughly. Dot the mixture with butter. Cover the dish and bake at 325 degrees for 90 minutes or until rice is tender and liquid absorbed.

TUNA ON TOAST

2 cans of tuna
1 cup of milk
2 tablespoons of butter
2 tablespoons of flour
¼ teaspoon of salt
Dash of pepper
Bread

Melt butter in a pan. Stir in flour, salt and a dash of pepper. Raise the heat and stir in the milk. Cook quickly and keep stirring until mixture thickens and bubbles. Remove the sauce from the heat. Stir tuna fish into the mixture and serve on toast.

VENISON & BLACK BEAN CHILI

1 pound of ground venison
28 ounces of canned black beans, drained
1 onion, diced
2 cups of water
6 ounces of tomato paste
3 cloves of garlic, diced
4 tablespoons of olive oil
1 tablespoon of chili powder
2 teaspoons of cumin
2 teaspoons of cocoa powder, unsweetened
½ teaspoon of cayenne pepper
½ teaspoon coriander
½ teaspoon cinnamon

In a big pot or Dutch oven, heat oil and sauté venison, onions and garlic until meat is browned. Stir in chili powder, cumin, cocoa powder, cayenne, coriander and cinnamon. Mix thoroughly. Add water and tomatoes and bring to a boil. Reduce heat and simmer for 30 minutes. Stir in the black beans and simmer for another 30 minutes.

WALLEYE STEW

5 pounds of walleye
3 quarts of water
2 cans of tomatoes
3 chopped onions
3 potatoes, diced
4 hard boiled eggs, diced
4 strips of bacon, diced
½ stick of butter
1 large can of tomato paste
1 tablespoon of Worcestershire sauce
Tabasco to taste

Cover fish with water and boil until tender. Remove fish, add all the ingredients and simmer for one hour. Bone the cooked fish and add to stew for the last five minutes of cooking. You can also make this recipe with similar tasting and textured fish.

WHITEFISH POINT WARMER

2 quarts of rum
2 quarts of water
1 quart of cognac
1 quart of lemon juice
6 ounces of peach brandy
¾ pound of sugar
Lake ice

In a large container, dissolve sugar in the water and stir in the lemon juice. Add the remaining ingredients. Drop in a big chunk of ice and allow it to cool the punch for 2 hours.

WILLAPA BAY STEW

2 cups of milk
10 ounces of oysters
1 cup of onion, diced
1 cup of celery, diced
1 cup of potato, diced
½ stick of butter
2 tablespoons of cornstarch
Salt and pepper to taste

In a pan sauté vegetables in the butter until they are tender. Dissolve the cornstarch in the milk then add the milk, oysters and seasoning to the pot. Simmer until the oysters are firm.

WINTER WARMING DINNER

2 pounds of beef, cubed
1 can of cream of mushroom soup
½ cup of red wine
4 ounces of whole mushrooms, canned
1 envelope of onion soup mix

In a slow cooker, combine all ingredients and mix thoroughly. Cook on low heat for 8 hours or on high heat for 5 hours.

For information on all of Tim Murphy's
cookbooks and his other titles visit
www.flanneljohn.com.